"

Building a home is about
creating a space that
reflects your soul,
where every corner tells your
story.

-Ulli Karner-

Ulli Karner

FOUNDER OF BACK TO BASICS

Ulli Karner, the visionary behind BACK to BASICS, is dedicated to simplifying the home-building process.

With her passion for creating functional and beautiful spaces, Ulli brings years of experience and expertise in construction, design, and project management.

Her goal is to guide individuals through the complexities of building their dream homes by offering practical advice and a step-by-step approach.

Through this workbook, Ulli shares her knowledge to help you make informed decisions and achieve a smooth, stress-free home-building experience.

CHAPTERS

INTRODUCTION

CHECK IN ADVANCE

- Inspiration and Research
- Budget and Financing
- Property Search

PLANNING & DESIGN

- Architecture and Style
- Materials and Construction
- Interior Design and Decoration

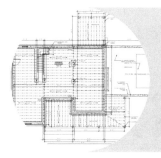

PERMITS & REGULATIONS

- Building Requirements
- Energy Efficiency and Environmental Standards

4

CHAPTERS CONT.

1

INTRODUCTION

BUILDING YOUR DREAM

Welcome to your ultimate guide for planning and executing the construction of your new home. This workbook is designed to help you navigate the entire process systematically and efficiently, from initial ideas and budgeting to selecting the right contractor and overseeing construction.

With detailed checklists, planning tools, and expert tips, you'll have everything you need to turn your dream home into a reality. Whether you're building from scratch or renovating, this workbook ensures you stay organized and informed every step of the way. Let's embark on this exciting journey together!

BUILDING YOUR DREAM HOME

16 STEPS TO YOUR DREAM HOME

Understanding the home building process involves navigating each stage, from planning and design to move-in. It includes budgeting, obtaining permits, selecting materials, overseeing construction, and making interior and exterior finishing decisions. Being familiar with these steps ensures smooth project management and helps turn your vision into reality.

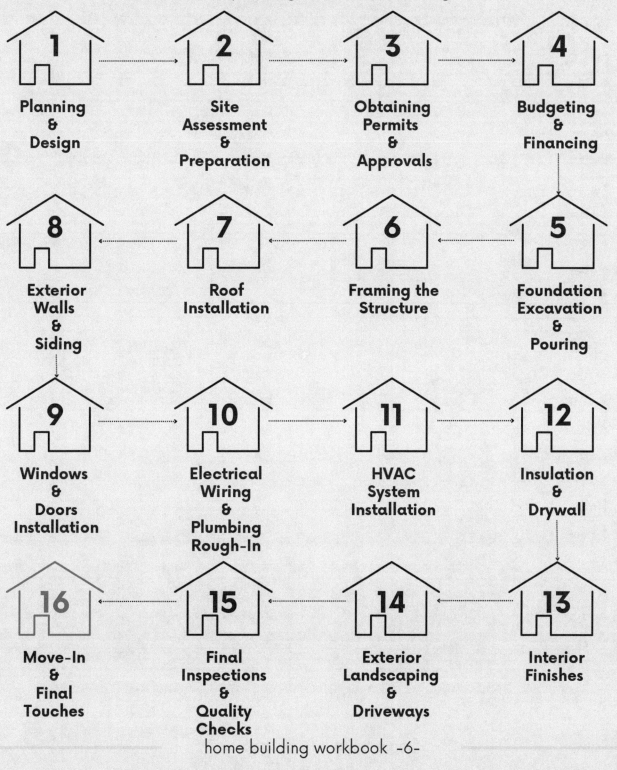

1 Planning & Design

2 Site Assessment & Preparation

3 Obtaining Permits & Approvals

4 Budgeting & Financing

8 Exterior Walls & Siding

7 Roof Installation

6 Framing the Structure

5 Foundation Excavation & Pouring

9 Windows & Doors Installation

10 Electrical Wiring & Plumbing Rough-In

11 HVAC System Installation

12 Insulation & Drywall

16 Move-In & Final Touches

15 Final Inspections & Quality Checks

14 Exterior Landscaping & Driveways

13 Interior Finishes

BUILDING YOUR DREAM HOME

CONTACT LIST

👤 Name
☎ Phone
✉ Email
🌐 Website
📍 Address
📋 Notes

👤 Name
☎ Phone
✉ Email
🌐 Website
📍 Address
📋 Notes

👤 Name
☎ Phone
✉ Email
🌐 Website
📍 Address
📋 Notes

👤 Name
☎ Phone
✉ Email
🌐 Website
📍 Address
📋 Notes

👤 Name
☎ Phone
✉ Email
🌐 Website
📍 Address
📋 Notes

👤 Name
☎ Phone
✉ Email
🌐 Website
📍 Address
📋 Notes

👤 Name
☎ Phone
✉ Email
🌐 Website
📍 Address
📋 Notes

👤 Name
☎ Phone
✉ Email
🌐 Website
📍 Address
📋 Notes

CHAPTER 2

CHECK IN ADVANCE

CHECKLIST

CHECK IN ADVANCE

This checklist helps you plan and execute the construction of your new home systematically and efficiently.

CHECK IN ADVANCE

1. Inspiration and Research

☐ Collect images and floor plans of your favorite houses (e.g., Cape Cod, Colonial, French Country, Craftsman)

☐ Study architecture magazines and websites (houzz.com, pinterest.com, bhg.com, dwell.com, etc.)

2. Budget and Financing

☐ Set the overall budget

☐ Review and apply for financing options in your area

3. Property Search

☐ Find a suitable plot of land

☐ Check local building regulations and soil conditions

☐ Calculate land development costs

NOTES

INSPIRATION & RESEARCH

Collect Images and Floor Plans

- **Explore Different Styles:** Start by familiarizing yourself with various architectural styles such as Cape Cod, Colonial, Ranch, and Craftsman. Each style has unique features and characteristics that might resonate with your vision.

- **Create a Vision Board:** Use tools like Pinterest, Houzz, or a physical board to gather images of exteriors, interiors, floor plans, and specific design elements that appeal to you. This visual compilation will help clarify your preferences and guide your discussions with architects and designers.

- **Download Floor Plans:** Look for floor plans that fit your needs and preferences. Consider the layout, number of rooms, and functional spaces. Save these plans as references when discussing possibilities with your architect.

Study Architecture Magazines and Websites

- **Architecture Magazines:** Subscribe to or browse through magazines like Architectural Digest, Better Homes & Gardens, and Dwell. These publications often feature a range of home styles, renovation ideas, and the latest trends in home design. Take notes on elements that stand out to you.

- **Online Resources:** Utilize websites like Houzz, Pinterest, and architectural blogs to gather ideas and inspiration. These platforms offer extensive galleries of home designs, floor plans, and user stories that can spark creativity and provide practical insights.

- **Read Case Studies:** Look for case studies or articles about home construction projects similar to what you envision. Understanding the challenges and solutions others have encountered can prepare you for your own project.

- **Virtual Tours:** Take advantage of virtual home tours available on many architectural websites. These tours offer a realistic view of different design elements and how they come together in a completed home.

- **Local Inspiration:** Don't forget to explore your local area. Visit open houses, model homes, and newly constructed neighborhoods to see design features and layouts in person.

INSPIRATION & RESEARCH

Compile Your Findings

- **Create a Scrapbook or Digital Folder:** Organize your collected images, floor plans, and notes into a scrapbook or a digital folder. Categorize them by style, room, or feature for easy reference.
- **Identify Common Themes:** As you compile your inspiration, identify common themes or elements that repeatedly catch your eye. These will be key to developing your own unique style.
- **Prepare for Professional Consultations:** Bring your scrapbook or digital collection to meetings with your architect, designer, and contractor. It will serve as a valuable tool to convey your vision and ensure everyone is on the same page.

Engaging in thorough inspiration and research sets a solid foundation for your home construction project, ensuring that your final design is both beautiful and functional, tailored to your tastes and needs.

BRAINSTORMING

Building Your Dream: Brainstorming Ideas for Your New Home

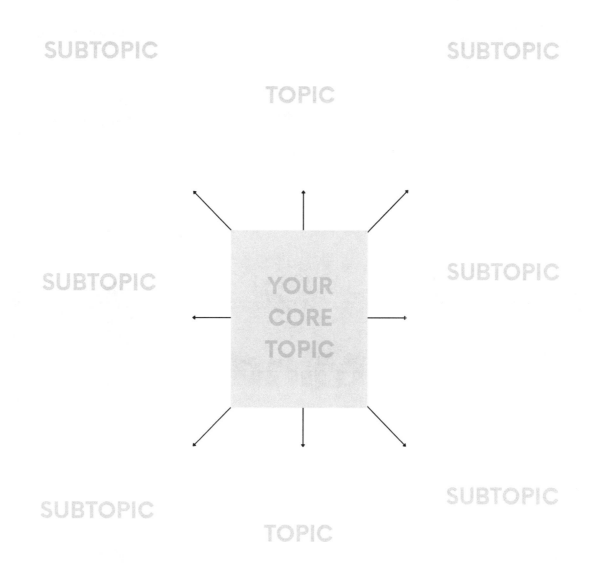

SUBTOPIC

SUBTOPIC

TOPIC

SUBTOPIC

SUBTOPIC

YOUR
CORE
TOPIC

SUBTOPIC

SUBTOPIC

TOPIC

NOTES

MIND MAP

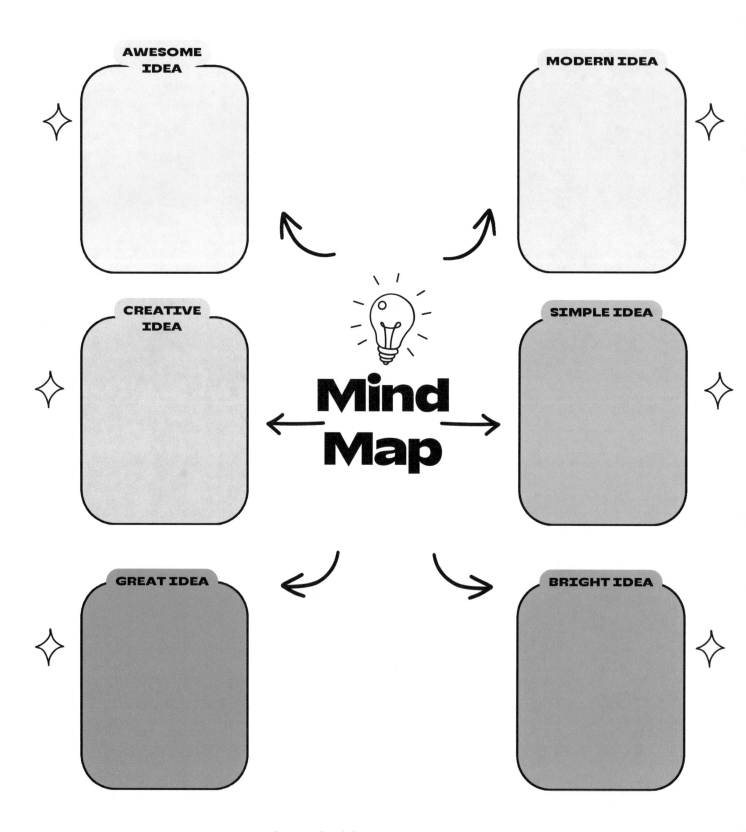

AWESOME IDEA

MODERN IDEA

CREATIVE IDEA

SIMPLE IDEA

Mind Map

GREAT IDEA

BRIGHT IDEA

NOTES

INSPIRATION & RESEARCH

WEBSITES TO REMEMBER

Home Design & Inspiration Websites:

_____

_____

Contractor & Builder Resources Websites:

_____

_____

Finance & Budgeting Websites:

_____

_____

House Plans & Architectural Resources Websites:

_____

_____

Interior Design & Decorating Websites:

_____

_____

Landscaping & Outdoor Design Websites:

_____

_____

Move-in Planning & Home Services Websites:

_____

_____

Other Websites:

_____

PASSWORD TRACKER

WEBSITE	LOGIN	PASSWORD
Notes:		
Notes:		
Notes:		
Notes:		
Notes:		
Notes:		
Notes:		
Notes:		
Notes:		
Notes:		

BUDGET & FINANCING

Set the Overall Budget

- **Initial Budget Planning:** Start by determining your total available funds, including savings and potential loans. Factor in all anticipated expenses, such as land purchase, construction costs, permits, and professional fees (e.g., architects, contractors).

- **Contingency Fund:** Allocate a contingency fund, typically 10-20% of your total budget, to cover unexpected expenses that may arise during the construction process.

- **Detailed Cost Breakdown:** Break down your budget into specific categories, such as land acquisition, site preparation, foundation, framing, roofing, electrical, plumbing, interior finishes, and landscaping. This will help you track expenses more accurately.

- **Cost Estimation Tools:** Use cost estimation tools and software, or consult with a financial advisor or builder, to get a realistic estimate of your project costs. Regularly update this as you get more precise quotes and information.

Review and Apply for Financing Options

- **Mortgage Loans:** Explore various mortgage loan options, such as fixed-rate, adjustable-rate, and construction-to-permanent loans. Each type has different terms, interest rates, and payment structures.

- **Construction Loans:** Consider a construction loan, which provides funds in stages as your home is built. These loans often convert to a traditional mortgage once construction is complete.

- **Government Programs:** Research government programs that offer incentives, grants, or low-interest loans for home construction, especially those promoting energy efficiency or sustainable building practices.

- **Comparing Lenders:** Shop around and compare offers from multiple lenders. Pay attention to interest rates, loan terms, fees, and repayment conditions.

- **Credit Check:** Ensure your credit score is in good standing, as it will affect your ability to secure favorable financing terms. Address any discrepancies or debts before applying.

- **Pre-Approval:** Obtain pre-approval from your chosen lender to streamline the loan process and demonstrate your financial readiness to contractors and sellers.

BUDGET & FINANCING

EXPENSE TRACKER

NR	DATE	DESCRIPTION	AMOUNT
		TOTAL:	

NOTES

BUDGET & FINANCING

PROPERTY SEARCH

Find a Suitable Plot of Land

- **Location Considerations:** Identify areas that meet your lifestyle needs and preferences, such as proximity to work, schools, amenities, and recreational activities. Consider future development plans in the area that might affect property value.
- **Land Listings:** Use real estate websites, local listings, and work with a real estate agent specializing in land sales to find available plots that match your criteria.
- **Site Visits:** Conduct site visits to evaluate the land's topography, natural features, and overall suitability for your planned home. Pay attention to access roads, utilities, and surrounding properties.

Check Local Building Regulations and Soil Conditions

- **Zoning Laws:** Verify the land's zoning regulations to ensure it is designated for residential use and check for any restrictions that may affect your construction plans (e.g., building height, setbacks, lot coverage).
- **Building Permits:** Understand the process and requirements for obtaining building permits in your area. This includes necessary documentation, fees, and the timeline for approval.
- **Soil Testing:** Conduct soil tests to assess the land's stability and suitability for construction. Poor soil conditions may require additional foundation work, increasing costs.
- **Environmental Assessments:** Check for any environmental regulations or protected areas that may impact your building plans. This includes wetlands, flood zones, and wildlife habitats.

PROPERTY SEARCH

Calculate Development Costs

- **Utility Connections:** Estimate the cost of connecting to utilities such as water, sewage, electricity, and gas. If utilities are not readily available, consider the expense of installing wells, septic systems, or alternative energy sources.
- **Site Preparation:** Account for site preparation costs, including clearing vegetation, grading, excavation, and drainage systems. These can vary significantly based on the land's condition and topography.
- **Access Roads and Driveways:** Factor in the costs of building access roads or driveways to ensure safe and convenient entry to your property.
- **Permits and Fees:** Include costs for all necessary permits and fees required for land development and construction. This may include building permits, impact fees, and inspection fees.
- **Landscaping and Exterior Work:** Plan for landscaping and exterior features such as fencing, walkways, and retaining walls, which can add to the overall development costs.

By carefully planning your budget and thoroughly researching financing options and land requirements, you can ensure a smoother, more predictable home construction process. These steps will help you stay within your financial limits and avoid costly surprises down the line.

NOTES

PROPERTY SEARCH

PLANNING & DESIGN

PLANNING AND DESIGN

This section ensures your home is designed to your specifications and meets all necessary standards.

**PLANNING
AND
DESIGN**

4. Architecture and Style

☐ Hire an architect with experience in your selected style
☐ Choose the desired style (e.g., Cape Cod, Colonial, Ranch, French Country, Craftsman)
☐ Create a floor plan together with the architect based on your ideas

5. Typical Features of Your House

☐ Large porches, terraces, or decks
☐ Open floor plans with live-in kitchen and fireplace
☐ Large windows and patio doors
☐ Gable roofs and dormer windows
☐ Traditional siding (e.g., wood shingles, brick)

6. Materials and Construction

☐ Select high-quality building materials available in your Area
☐ Timber frame construction with wood-based panels
☐ Ensure energy efficiency and insulation to meet standards

7. Interior Design and Decoration

☐ Design interiors in the your prefered style (e.g., open living areas, kitchen islands, built-in shelves, wainscoting)
☐ Choose flooring (e.g., hardwood, carpet)
☐ Include typical details like fireplaces, grand staircases, and spacious bathrooms

PLANNING AND DESIGN

Hire an Architect Experienced in the Desired Style

- **Specialized Expertise:** Select an architect who has experience designing homes in the style you prefer, whether it's Cape Cod, Colonial, Ranch, or Craftsman. Their familiarity with the aesthetic and structural nuances of your chosen style will ensure that your vision is accurately captured.

- **Portfolio Review:** Ask to see the architect's portfolio of similar projects to assess their previous work. This will give you an idea of their design capabilities and how well they execute the desired style.

- **Consultations and Collaboration:** During the design process, collaborate closely with the architect to ensure that your personal preferences, lifestyle needs, and functional requirements are integrated into the design. Open communication will help translate your ideas into a cohesive plan.

Choose a Style (e.g., Cape Cod, Colonial, Ranch, Craftsman)

- **Cape Cod:** Known for its symmetrical design, steep roofs, dormer windows, and modest size, this style is ideal for those seeking a cozy, traditional look.

- **Colonial:** Featuring a more formal, rectangular design with a central entrance and evenly spaced windows, Colonial homes often incorporate columns and elaborate details, giving them a stately appearance.

- **Ranch:** A single-story layout with an open, flowing floor plan, Ranch homes are characterized by their sprawling design and close connection to the surrounding landscape, often including large windows and sliding glass doors.

- **Craftsman:** Celebrated for its handcrafted details, low-pitched roofs, and deep front porches, the Craftsman style emphasizes natural materials like wood and stone and often features exposed beams and built-in furniture.

Each of these styles offers unique design elements and architectural features that cater to different tastes and practical needs. Understanding the distinct characteristics of each will help you select the right style for your home.

PLANNING AND DESIGN

Create a Floor Plan Based on Preferred Models

- **Functional Layout:** Once you've chosen your desired style, work with your architect to develop a floor plan that balances form and function. The floor plan should reflect how you envision living in the space—whether you prefer an open-concept design for social gatherings or defined rooms for privacy.

- **Incorporate Signature Elements:** Make sure the floor plan includes signature features of your chosen style, such as large verandas in Craftsman homes, open living areas in Ranch-style homes, or central hallways in Colonial designs.

- **Customization:** Tailor the floor plan to meet your specific needs, whether it's adding extra bedrooms, a home office, or a larger kitchen. Flexibility in the design phase will ensure the home meets both your current and future requirements.

- **Consider Future Expansion:** Plan for future expansions, such as adding a second floor or extending living areas, by designing the layout with potential growth in mind. A well-thought-out floor plan allows for adaptability over time.

By carefully selecting your architectural style and working with an experienced architect to create a floor plan that reflects your preferences, you can ensure that your home is both visually appealing and practical for everyday living.

PLANNING AND DESIGN

Typical Features of Your Home - Large Porches, Terraces, or Decks

- **Outdoor Living:** Homes with expansive porches, terraces, or decks offer extended outdoor living spaces that are perfect for relaxation, entertaining, and enjoying nature. These areas can serve as an outdoor dining space, a cozy seating area, or a place for family activities.
- **Covered vs. Uncovered:** Large covered porches provide shelter from the elements, making them usable year-round, while open decks and terraces create sunny spaces ideal for barbecues, lounging, or gardening.
- **Architectural Focal Point:** Porches and decks often become a focal point in the overall design of the home, enhancing its curb appeal and providing a welcoming entrance.

Open Floor Plans with Live-In Kitchen and Fireplace

- **Seamless Flow:** An open floor plan connects the kitchen, dining, and living areas, creating a spacious and airy environment. This layout promotes family interaction and is ideal for hosting social gatherings, as there's no barrier between spaces.
- **Live-In Kitchen:** A live-in kitchen typically includes a central island or breakfast bar, providing a multifunctional area for cooking, dining, and socializing. This design makes the kitchen the heart of the home.
- **Fireplace:** A central fireplace in the living or dining area adds warmth and ambiance. Whether traditional or modern, the fireplace serves as a cozy focal point in open-plan living, making the space feel inviting and comfortable.

PLANNING AND DESIGN

Large Windows and Patio Doors

- **Natural Light:** Large windows and patio doors are designed to bring in plenty of natural light, creating a bright and welcoming interior. They also provide expansive views of the outdoors, blending the interior and exterior spaces.

- **Indoor-Outdoor Connection:** Patio doors, especially sliding or French doors, make it easy to move between indoor living areas and outdoor patios or decks, enhancing the flow of the home and encouraging outdoor living.

- **Energy Efficiency:** Modern windows often include energy-efficient features such as double glazing or low-E coatings, helping to reduce heating and cooling costs while maintaining a comfortable indoor environment.

Gable Roofs and Dormer Windows

- **Classic Architectural Element:** Gable roofs, characterized by their triangular shape, are a hallmark of traditional home designs like Cape Cod or Colonial. They offer practical benefits such as efficient water drainage and additional attic space.

- **Dormer Windows:** Dormer windows are small, roofed structures that extend from a gable roof, adding both light and space to upper floors. Dormers create charming architectural interest and can provide functional headroom in attic spaces or lofts.

- **Aesthetic Appeal:** Gable roofs and dormers contribute to the classic, timeless aesthetic of a home, while also adding character and dimension to the exterior.

PLANNING AND DESIGN

Traditional Siding (e.g., Wood Shingles, Brick)

- **Natural Materials:** Traditional siding materials like wood shingles or brick are often chosen for their durability and authentic, natural appearance. Wood siding, in particular, gives a warm and rustic charm, while brick offers a more solid and timeless look.

- **Longevity and Maintenance:** Both wood shingles and brick are known for their longevity, though they require different levels of maintenance. Wood may need regular staining or sealing, while brick requires less upkeep but can be more expensive upfront.

- **Curb Appeal:** The choice of siding plays a major role in defining the overall aesthetic of your home. Whether you prefer the coastal feel of wood shingles or the stately presence of brick, traditional siding materials enhance the visual impact of your house.

These typical features contribute to the distinctive style, functionality, and beauty of your home, creating a space that is both visually appealing and tailored to modern living.

PLANNING AND DESIGN

Select High-Quality Building Materials Available in Your Area

- **Local Availability:** It's essential to choose building materials that are readily available in your region. This not only ensures that your project stays on schedule but also helps to reduce transportation costs. Local materials are often better suited to the climate, ensuring long-term durability and performance.

- **Sustainable Options:** Consider using eco-friendly materials, such as sustainably sourced wood, recycled metals, or composite materials. These not only reduce the environmental footprint of your build but also align with modern green building standards.

- **Durability and Aesthetics:** High-quality materials like stone, brick, or premium-grade wood add durability and aesthetic appeal. Opting for durable materials can increase the longevity of your home and reduce long-term maintenance costs.

Timber Frame Construction with Wood-Based Panels

- **Lightweight and Versatile:** Timber frame construction, combined with wood-based panels such as OSB (Oriented Strand Board) or plywood, is a popular choice for many home builds. This method allows for flexibility in design and offers the advantage of quick construction compared to traditional masonry.

- **Sustainable and Renewable:** Timber is a renewable resource, making it an environmentally friendly option. Timber frame homes can be highly energy-efficient, and the use of wood-based panels adds structural integrity while minimizing waste.

- **Insulation-Friendly:** Wood is a natural insulator, and the timber frame construction method allows for easy incorporation of modern insulation materials, helping maintain the building's energy efficiency.

PLANNING AND DESIGN

Ensure Energy Efficiency and Insulation to Meet Standards

- **Meeting Building Codes:** In most regions, there are stringent energy efficiency standards that must be met. Proper insulation is critical to ensuring that your home stays warm in the winter and cool in the summer, while also reducing your energy consumption.

- **Insulation Materials:** Use high-performance insulation materials like rigid foam, spray foam, or mineral wool. These materials improve thermal performance and contribute to a home's overall energy efficiency. It's important to insulate walls, roofs, and floors effectively to avoid heat loss.

- **Sealing and Ventilation:** Proper sealing of doors, windows, and any other openings is crucial to prevent drafts and energy loss. However, ventilation should also be considered to maintain air quality and prevent moisture buildup. Advanced HVAC systems, along with proper insulation, can make your home highly energy-efficient.

- **Sustainability and Cost Savings:** Energy-efficient homes not only reduce environmental impact but also offer long-term cost savings. By using quality insulation and ensuring your home meets or exceeds energy standards, you'll benefit from lower utility bills and a more comfortable living environment year-round.

By selecting the right materials, using sustainable timber frame construction, and focusing on energy efficiency, your home will be well-prepared for durability, sustainability, and cost-effective performance.

PLANNING AND DESIGN

Design Interiors in Your Preferred Style

- **Open Living Areas:** Modern homes often feature open-plan designs that combine the kitchen, dining, and living spaces into one seamless area. This layout promotes social interaction and creates a more spacious, airy feel. It's perfect for entertaining and family gatherings.

- **Kitchen Islands:** A kitchen island is both a functional and aesthetic centerpiece. It provides extra counter space for meal preparation, additional storage, and seating options. Islands can be customized with features like sinks, cooktops, or breakfast bars to enhance usability.

- **Built-in Shelves and Wainscoting:** Incorporating built-in shelving units adds practical storage and a custom, finished look to living rooms, libraries, and bedrooms. Wainscoting, which is a decorative paneling applied to the lower half of walls, adds classic elegance to dining rooms, hallways, and entryways, giving your home a more polished and traditional feel.

Choose Flooring

- **Hardwood:** Hardwood floors are a timeless choice that adds warmth, durability, and natural beauty to any room. They come in a wide range of wood species, finishes, and stain colors to complement various interior styles. Hardwood floors are easy to maintain and age beautifully over time.

- **Carpet:** For a cozier feel, carpet can be used in bedrooms, living rooms, or family rooms. It provides a soft, comfortable surface underfoot and helps with sound insulation. Carpets come in a variety of textures, colors, and patterns, allowing for personalization and comfort in private areas of the home.

- **Other Options:** Consider alternatives like luxury vinyl, tile, or stone for areas such as kitchens, bathrooms, and mudrooms. These materials offer high durability and are often easier to clean and maintain, making them ideal for high-traffic or moisture-prone areas.

PLANNING AND DESIGN

Include Typical Details Like Fireplaces, Grand Staircases, and Spacious Bathrooms, Vaulted Ceilings, Smart Home Features, ...

- **Fireplaces:** A fireplace is both a functional heating source and a striking architectural feature. Whether you choose a traditional wood-burning fireplace or a modern gas or electric version, it creates a cozy atmosphere and serves as a focal point in living rooms, family rooms, or even bedrooms.

- **Grand Staircases:** Large, sweeping staircases add a touch of luxury and elegance to your home's entrance or central hall. Whether crafted from wood or metal, staircases can be custom-designed with decorative balustrades and rails to match your interior style.

- **Spacious Bathrooms:** Large bathrooms with features like double vanities, soaking tubs, and walk-in showers create a spa-like experience in your home. Ample storage, elegant fixtures, and premium materials such as marble or ceramic tiles elevate the look and functionality of the space.

- **Vaulted ceilings** are a popular architectural feature that can dramatically enhance the appearance and ambiance of your home. They create a sense of spaciousness and luxury by elevating the height of the room, making the space feel open and airy.

- **Smart home features** integrate technology to make daily living more convenient, energy-efficient, and secure. Popular options include:
  - Smart Lighting: Automate lighting with apps or voice commands.
  - Thermostat Control: Adjust heating and cooling remotely to optimize comfort and energy savings.
  - Security Systems: Smart locks, cameras, and alarms provide enhanced home security.
  - Appliance Automation: Control appliances like ovens, washers, and speakers from your phone.

These features add modern convenience, improve energy efficiency, and offer peace of mind.

These interior design and decoration choices not only reflect your personal style but also enhance the overall functionality and comfort of your home. By incorporating thoughtful design elements and high-quality materials, you create living spaces that are both beautiful and practical.

PLANNING AND DESIGN

When selecting a color palette for a new home, it's essential to consider various factors to create a harmonious and visually appealing environment. Here's a detailed breakdown of what to keep in mind:

Architectural Style

- **Traditional vs. Modern:** Some colors work better with specific architectural styles. For example, muted tones may suit Colonial or Craftsman homes, while bold, minimalist palettes fit modern or contemporary designs.

Home Size and Scale

- **Smaller Homes:** Lighter colors can make smaller spaces feel larger and airier.
- **Larger Homes:** Darker shades can add warmth and make expansive areas feel more intimate.

Lighting Conditions

- **Natural Light:** Consider how much natural light each room receives. North-facing rooms may need warmer colors to counteract cooler light, while south-facing rooms can handle cooler shades.
- **Artificial Light:** The type of light bulbs used (LED, incandescent) can also affect how paint colors appear.

Exterior vs. Interior Colors

- **Exterior Colors:** Choose hues that blend with the surroundings, neighborhood, and architectural style. The exterior often includes multiple elements like siding, trim, doors, and accents.
- **Interior Colors:** Think about flow between rooms and how one space transitions into another.

Accent and Trim Colors

- Accent colors can enhance architectural details like trim, doors, window frames, and shutters. Trim colors are typically neutral (white, black, or beige) but can also be used to create contrast with bolder accent colors.

PLANNING AND DESIGN

Room Functionality
- **Living Spaces:** Opt for calming, neutral tones in living rooms and bedrooms to promote relaxation.
- **Kitchens and Bathrooms:** Brighter, fresher tones like whites, blues, or greens are often used for a clean, vibrant feel.

Personal Preferences
- Reflect your personality and preferences through color choices, whether that's vibrant and bold or soft and subdued.

Color Trends
- Stay updated on current color trends, but ensure that choices remain timeless and don't become quickly outdated.

Material Coordination
- Coordinate paint colors with other design elements, such as flooring, cabinetry, countertops, and furniture, to ensure everything works together.

Long-Term Durability
- Consider how exterior colors may weather over time and how interior shades might change due to wear and tear, or sunlight exposure.

By carefully considering these elements, you can select a color palette that enhances the beauty, functionality, and overall atmosphere of your home.

PLANNING AND DESIGN

PROJECT SCHEDULE

DATE :

PROJECT:

MONTH 1

MONTH 2

MONTH 3

MONTH 4

MONTH 5

PLANNING AND DESIGN

INTERIOR PAINT SELECTION

Room Name, Size (sq. ft.) and Function:

Primary Color:

Color Name:

Color Code & Finish:

Manufacturer & Price:

Room Name, Size (sq. ft.) and Function:

Primary Color:

Color Name:

Color Code & Finish:

Manufacturer & Price:

Room Name, Size (sq. ft.) and Function:

Primary Color:

Color Name:

Color Code & Finish:

Manufacturer & Price:

Room Name, Size (sq. ft.) and Function:

Primary Color:

Color Name:

Color Code & Finish:

Manufacturer & Price:

INTERIOR PAINT SELECTION CONT.

Room Name, Size (sq. ft.) and Function:

Primary Color:

Color Name:

Color Code & Finish:

Manufacturer & Price:

Room Name, Size (sq. ft.) and Function:

Primary Color:

Color Name:

Color Code & Finish:

Manufacturer & Price:

Room Name, Size (sq. ft.) and Function:

Primary Color:

Color Name:

Color Code & Finish:

Manufacturer & Price:

Room Name, Size (sq. ft.) and Function:

Primary Color:

Color Name:

Color Code & Finish:

Manufacturer & Price:

INTERIOR MATERIAL SELECTION

Interior Door Selection

Size & Style: Hardware:

Door Material: Door Color:

Glass Type: Grill Pattern:

Manufacturer & Price:

Cabinet Selection

Door Style: Hardware Style & Finish:

Door Material: Crown Molding:

Color Code & Finish:

Manufacturer & Price:

Countertop Selection

Material: Size:

Product Name:

Edge:

Manufacturer & Price:

Backsplash Selection

Material: Size:

Product Name:

Color & Grout Color:

Manufacturer & Price:

INTERIOR MATERIAL SELECTION

Flooring Selection

Material: Size:

Product Name:

Color:

Manufacturer & Price:

Tile Selection

Material: Size:

Product Name: Crown Molding:

Color & Finish:

Manufacturer & Price:

Lighting Selection

Material:

Product Name:

Color & Finish:

Manufacturer & Price:

Plumbing Selection

Material:

Product Name:

Color & Finish:

Manufacturer & Price:

EXTERIOR PAINT SELECTION

Siding Paint Selection

Primary Color:

Color Name:

Color Code & Finish:

Manufacturer & Price:

Trim Paint Selection

Primary Color:

Color Name:

Color Code & Finish:

Manufacturer & Price:

Soffit Paint Selection

Primary Color:

Color Name:

Color Code & Finish:

Manufacturer & Price:

Fascia Paint Selection

Primary Color:

Color Name:

Color Code & Finish:

Manufacturer & Price:

EXTERIOR MATERIAL SELECTION

Masonary Selection

Stone Color: Brick Color:

Color Name: Color Name:

Color Code & Finish: Color Code & Finish:

Manufacturer & Price: Manufacturer & Price:

Column Selection

Column Style:

Column Color Name:

Color Code & Finish:

Manufacturer & Price:

Roofing Selection

Material & Style:

Roofing Name:

Color Code & Finish:

Manufacturer & Price:

Gutter & Spout Selection

Material:

Size:

Color Code & Finish:

Manufacturer & Price:

EXTERIOR MATERIAL SELECTION

Window Selection

Size & Style: Hardware:

Frame Material: Frame Color:

Glass Type: Grill Pattern:

Manufacturer & Price:

Patio Door Selection

Size & Style: Hardware:

Frame Material: Frame Color:

Glass Type: Grill Pattern:

Manufacturer & Price:

Blinds Selection

Material & Style:

Product Name:

Color Code & Finish:

Manufacturer & Price:

Shutter Selection

Material:

Size:

Color Code & Finish:

Manufacturer & Price:

PLANNING AND DESIGN

EXTERIOR MATERIAL SELECTION

Entrance Door Selection

Size & Style: Hardware:

Door Material: Door Color:

Glass Type: Grill Pattern:

Manufacturer & Price:

Garage Door Selection

Size & Style: Hardware:

Door Material: Door Color:

Glass Type: Grill Pattern:

Manufacturer & Price:

Railings & Fence Selection

Material & Style:

Product Name:

Color Code & Finish:

Manufacturer & Price:

Exterior Light Selection

Material & Style:

Product Name:

Color Code & Finish:

Manufacturer & Price:

CHAPTER 4

PERMITS & REGULATIONS

PERMITS AND REGULATIONS

This checklist helps you plan and execute the construction of your new home systematically and efficiently.

8. Building Requirements

☐ Obtain building permits from the local authority

☐ Comply with building codes and energy efficiency standards

☐ Make any necessary adjustments to meet your local regulations

☐ Submit Detailed Plans

9. Energy Efficiency and Environmental Standards

☐ Consider passive house standards

☐ Integrate sustainable materials and technologies

☐ Environmental Considerations

Secure all required building permits from your local municipality before starting construction. This typically includes permits for construction, electrical, plumbing, and HVAC systems.

Provide detailed architectural plans, including site plans, floor plans, and elevation drawings, to the local building department for approval.

Depending on the location and scale of your project, you may need environmental permits, such as stormwater management permits or tree removal permits.

NOTES

PERMITS AND REGULATIONS

Navigating the permits and regulations process can be complex and time-consuming, but adhering to these guidelines ensures your project meets all legal requirements and standards for safety, quality, and environmental responsibility.

Building Permits

- **Obtain Necessary Permits:** Secure all required building permits from your local municipality before starting construction. This typically includes permits for construction, electrical, plumbing, and HVAC systems.

- **Submit Detailed Plans:** Provide detailed architectural plans, including site plans, floor plans, and elevation drawings, to the local building department for approval.

- **Environmental Considerations:** Depending on the location and scale of your project, you may need environmental permits, such as stormwater management permits or tree removal permits.

Zoning Regulations

- **Zoning Compliance:** Ensure your project complies with local zoning ordinances, which dictate land use, building height, setbacks, and density. You may need to apply for zoning variances if your project does not conform to these regulations.
- **Historic Districts:** If your property is in a historic district, you may need special approval from a historic preservation board, including design reviews to ensure the new construction aligns with the historical character of the area.

Safety and Building Codes

- **Adherence to Building Codes:** Follow the International Building Code (IBC), International Residential Code (IRC), and any state or local building codes. These codes govern structural integrity, fire safety, accessibility, and energy efficiency.

PERMITS AND REGULATIONS

Safety and Building Codes cont,

- **Inspections:** Schedule and pass various inspections at different stages of construction (e.g., foundation, framing, electrical, plumbing) to ensure compliance with building codes. Inspections are typically required before moving on to the next phase of construction.

Energy Efficiency and Environmental Standards

- **Energy Code Compliance:** Adhere to local energy codes, which may include specific insulation requirements, energy-efficient windows, and HVAC systems to reduce energy consumption and improve sustainability.

- **Environmental Impact Assessments:** Depending on the scale and location of your project, you may need to conduct environmental impact assessments (EIAs) to identify and mitigate any potential adverse effects on the environment.

Utilities and Infrastructure

- **Utility Permits:** Obtain permits for connecting to public utilities such as water, sewer, gas, and electricity. This often involves coordination with local utility companies.

- **Impact Fees:** Be aware of any impact fees that may be assessed by local governments to cover the cost of additional public services and infrastructure required by new development.

Neighborhood and Community

- **HOA Approval:** If your property is in a neighborhood governed by a Homeowners Association (HOA), you may need approval for your building plans from the HOA, including adherence to architectural guidelines and aesthetic standards.

PERMITS AND REGULATIONS

Neighborhood and Community Cont,

- **Public Hearings:** Some projects, particularly those requiring variances or located in sensitive areas, may require public hearings where neighbors and community members can express their support or concerns.

Documentation and Record Keeping

- **Maintain Records:** Keep thorough records of all permits, approvals, inspections, and communications with regulatory agencies. This documentation will be crucial for resolving any disputes and for future property sales or refinancing.

Final Approval and Occupancy

- **Certificate of Occupancy:** After completing construction and passing all required inspections, obtain a Certificate of Occupancy (CO) from your local building department. This document certifies that the building is safe and habitable.

- **Post-Construction Inspections:** Some jurisdictions may require additional post-construction inspections to ensure that all work complies with the approved plans and regulations.

NOTES

PERMITS AND REGULATIONS

PERMITS AND REGULATIONS

Consider Passive House Standards

- **Understanding Passive House:** Passive House standards are a set of rigorous energy efficiency criteria aimed at reducing a building's ecological footprint. They focus on maximizing the use of natural energy sources and minimizing energy losses.

- **Benefits:** Homes built to Passive House standards typically consume up to 90% less heating and cooling energy than conventional buildings. This translates to significant cost savings and a more comfortable living environment.

- **Key Features:** Key features of Passive House design include super-insulation, airtight construction, high-performance windows and doors, and mechanical ventilation systems with heat recovery. These elements work together to maintain a stable indoor temperature year-round with minimal energy input.

- **Implementation:** Work with an architect or builder experienced in Passive House design. Ensure your project incorporates elements like thermal bridge-free construction, optimized insulation levels, and orientation for natural sunlight.

Integrate Sustainable Materials and Technologies

- **Sustainable Materials:** Choose materials that are sustainably sourced, have a low environmental impact, and promote health and well-being within the home. Examples include:
  - **Recycled Materials:** Utilize recycled or repurposed materials for flooring, countertops, and structural elements.

  - **Renewable Resources:** Opt for materials made from renewable resources, such as bamboo flooring or wool insulation.

  - **Low VOC Products:** Select paints, adhesives, and finishes with low volatile organic compound (VOC) content to improve indoor air quality.

PERMITS AND REGULATIONS

Integrate Sustainable Materials and Technologies, Cont.

- **Energy-Efficient Technologies:** Incorporate advanced technologies to enhance energy efficiency and reduce your home's carbon footprint. These can include:
  - **Solar Panels:** Install photovoltaic panels to generate renewable energy and reduce reliance on grid electricity.

  - **Energy-Efficient Appliances:** Choose appliances with high energy efficiency ratings (e.g., ENERGY STAR) to lower energy consumption.

  - **Smart Home Systems:** Implement smart home systems to optimize energy usage. Automated thermostats, lighting controls, and energy monitoring systems can significantly reduce energy waste.

- **Water Conservation:** Integrate water-saving technologies and practices to reduce water usage. Low-flow fixtures, dual-flush toilets, and rainwater harvesting systems are effective options.

- **Insulation and Sealing:** Ensure that your home is well-insulated and properly sealed to prevent energy loss. This includes using high-quality insulation in walls, roofs, and floors, and sealing gaps around windows, doors, and other openings.

- **Green Building Certifications:** Consider pursuing green building certifications such as LEED (Leadership in Energy and Environmental Design) or BREEAM (Building Research Establishment Environmental Assessment Method). These certifications provide frameworks for achieving high standards of sustainability and energy efficiency.

By prioritizing energy efficiency and environmental standards, you not only create a more sustainable and cost-effective home but also contribute to a healthier planet. These considerations will ensure that your home is future-proofed, environmentally friendly, and economical to run.

NOTES

ENERGY EFFICIENCY

5

CHAPTER

CONSTRUCTION PHASE

CONSTRUCTION PHASE

This overview for the construction phase ensures your project is completed on time, within budget, and to the highest quality standards.

10. Construction Company

- [ ] Select a construction company experienced in building your desired home style. Look for a company with positive reviews, a strong portfolio, and appropriate licensing and insurance.
- [ ] Obtain and compare quotes from multiple companies.
- [ ] Sign a detailed construction contract that outlines all aspects of the project, including costs, payment schedules, timelines, materials, and responsibilities.

11. Construction Supervision

- [ ] Site Visits: Make regular site visits to monitor progress
- [ ] Quality Control: Verify that the construction aligns with architectural plans and building codes. Check that materials used match those specified and that workmanship meets quality standards.
  Ensure construction aligns with plans and specifications
- [ ] Timeline and Budget Monitoring: Keep track of the construction schedule and budget. Address any delays or cost overruns promptly to avoid impacting the overall timeline and financial plan.

You can also hire a professional for Construction Supervision

NOTES

CONSTRUCTION PHASE

Following these steps ensures you select a reputable contractor who meets your project needs and delivers quality work within your budget and timeline.

Finding Reputable Contractors

- **Referrals:** Ask friends, family, neighbors, and colleagues for recommendations. Personal experiences can provide trustworthy insights into a contractor's reliability and quality of work.
- **Online Reviews:** Check reviews on websites like Yelp, Google, and Angie's List. Look for contractors with consistently high ratings and read both positive and negative reviews to get a balanced perspective.
- **Professional Organizations:** Contact professional associations like the National Association of Home Builders (NAHB) or your local builders' association. These organizations often have directories of certified contractors who adhere to industry standards.

Obtaining Detailed Quotes

- **Request Quotes:** Contact at least four contractors to request detailed quotes. Provide each contractor with the same project specifications to ensure you receive comparable estimates.
- **Itemized Breakdown:** Ask for an itemized breakdown of costs, including materials, labor, permits, and any additional fees. This helps identify where each contractor allocates resources and ensures transparency.

Evaluating Quotes

- **Compare Costs:** Look for significant differences in pricing. Extremely low bids might indicate subpar materials or workmanship, while very high bids could suggest overpricing.
- **Timeline and Payment Schedule:** Review the proposed timeline and payment schedule. Ensure it aligns with your expectations and budget.
- **Scope of Work:** Ensure each quote includes a clear scope of work. This should detail the tasks to be performed, materials to be used, and any specific project requirements.

CONSTRUCTION PHASE

Checking Licenses and Insurance

- **Licensing:** Verify that the contractor holds a valid license to operate in your area. This can often be done through your state's licensing board or online databases.
- **Insurance:** Ensure the contractor has adequate insurance, including general liability and workers' compensation. This protects you from liability in case of accidents or damage during the project.

Reviewing Previous Work

- **Portfolio:** Ask to see a portfolio of the contractor's previous projects. Look for work that matches the style and scale of your project.
- **References:** Request references from recent clients. Contact them to ask about their experiences, the quality of work, and if there were any issues during the project.

Key Elements to Include in Your Contract

- **Project Description:** Provide a detailed description of the work to be performed, including materials, timelines, and specific tasks.
- **Payment Terms:** Clearly outline the payment schedule, including deposit, milestone payments, and final payment. Avoid contractors who demand a large upfront payment.
- **Timeline:** Specify start and completion dates. Include provisions for handling delays and extensions.
- **Change Orders:** Detail the process for handling changes to the project scope, including how costs and timelines will be adjusted.
- **Warranty:** Include information on warranties for workmanship and materials. Ensure you understand what is covered and the duration of the warranty.
- **Dispute Resolution:** Outline a process for resolving disputes, such as mediation or arbitration, to avoid lengthy legal battles.

CONTRACTOR CHECKLIST

Selecting the right contractor is essential for the success of your home construction project. This section of the workbook helps you through the process of comparing four different contractors, ensuring you make an informed decision.

CONTRACTOR 1

CONTRACTOR 2

CONTRACTOR 3

CONTRACTOR 4

CONSTRUCTION PHASE

Site Visits

- **Regular Monitoring:** Frequent site visits are essential to stay updated on the progress of your construction project. Regular check-ins allow you to see firsthand how the work is progressing, identify any potential issues early, and ensure that everything is on track.
- **Document Changes:** During your visits, take photos and notes to document progress. These records are useful for comparing the current state of the project with the original plans and identifying deviations or delays.

Quality Control

- **Plan Compliance:** It's crucial to verify that the construction is following the architectural plans, blueprints, and engineering specifications. Ensuring that structural elements, layouts, and features match the approved design helps prevent costly errors or rework later.
- **Building Code Adherence:** Ensure that the construction complies with local building codes and regulations, including safety, zoning, and energy efficiency standards. If non-compliance is found, it could result in delays or fines.
- **Material Verification:** Confirm that the materials used on-site match the specifications in your contract. Check for quality and durability, ensuring that substandard materials are not substituted.
- **Workmanship Standards:** Assess the quality of craftsmanship by inspecting key areas like framing, insulation, plumbing, and electrical work. Ensure that everything is completed with attention to detail and adheres to industry best practices.

CONSTRUCTION PHASE

Ensure Construction Aligns with Plans and Specifications

- **Consistency with Design:** Constantly review the progress to make sure the construction matches both the structural and aesthetic specifications. Verify that the layout, finishing, and design features—like window placements, room sizes, and structural details—are implemented as planned.
- **Addressing Deviations:** If any discrepancies are noticed between the actual build and the plans, address them immediately with the contractor to avoid compounded errors or miscommunications.

Timeline and Budget Monitoring

- **Stay on Schedule:** Track the construction timeline carefully to ensure that the project stays on schedule. Be proactive in addressing any delays, whether due to material shortages, weather issues, or labor availability. Regular meetings with the contractor help to adjust plans as needed.
- **Monitor Budget:** Keep an eye on expenses to avoid budget overruns. Ensure that any cost changes are approved before moving forward and maintain clear communication with the contractor on financial status. This helps manage cash flow and prevents unexpected financial burdens.
- **Resolve Issues Promptly:** If delays or cost overruns occur, address them quickly to minimize their impact on the overall project. Work closely with the contractor to find solutions, such as adjusting the schedule or reallocating resources, while keeping quality intact.

Effective construction supervision ensures that your project stays on track, both in terms of quality and efficiency, helping to avoid delays, additional costs, or compromises in the final build.

NOTES

CONSTRUCTION PHASE

POST CONSTRUCTION

POST CONSTRUCTION

This phase ensures your new home is ready for occupancy and well-maintained in the future.

POST
CONSTRUCTION

12. Interior Finishing and Decoration

☐ Choose furnishings in your desired style
☐ Select decor elements like curtains, rugs, and wall art
☐ Complete electrical and plumbing final works

13. Exterior Landscaping

☐ Plan garden design (e.g., lawn, flower beds, trees)
☐ Build terraces, decks, and driveways

14. Final Inspection and Move-In

☐ Conduct a final inspection of the house
☐ Address any deficiencies
☐ Plan and organize the move-in

15. After Move-In

☐ Create a maintenance plan for the house and garden
☐ Obtain insurance (home, liability, etc.)
☐ Get to know the neighborhood and your local community

NOTES

POST CONSTRUCTION

Choose Furnishings in Your Desired Style

- **Furniture Selection:** Picking furniture that complements your home's design is crucial for creating a cohesive and inviting space. Whether your style is modern, traditional, rustic, or eclectic, choose pieces that fit the room dimensions, flow with your home's overall aesthetic, and offer both functionality and comfort. Invest in key items like sofas, dining tables, and beds, focusing on quality and durability.

- **Customization:** Consider custom-made furniture if you're looking for unique pieces that perfectly match your vision. Built-in storage solutions, custom cabinetry, or bespoke furniture can help optimize space while aligning with your desired style.

Select Decor Elements Like Curtains, Rugs, and Wall Art

- **Window Treatments:** Curtains, blinds, or shutters not only provide privacy and control natural light but also play a significant role in enhancing the look of a room. Select fabrics and designs that complement your home's color scheme and architectural style. For a modern look, opt for minimalistic roller shades; for a more traditional approach, go for heavy, luxurious drapes.

- **Rugs and Carpets:** Rugs help define spaces, add warmth, and introduce texture and color to your interior. Choose area rugs that align with the size of your room and style preferences—whether you prefer a patterned rug for a statement piece or a neutral one to ground the space. Consider durability and material, especially in high-traffic areas.

- **Wall Art and Accessories:** Personalize your home with art that reflects your taste and personality. Large wall pieces, photo galleries, or framed artwork can add depth and interest to bare walls. Mirrors can enhance light and make spaces feel bigger. Don't overlook smaller decor items like vases, sculptures, or decorative objects that tie your theme together.

POST CONSTRUCTION

Complete Electrical and Plumbing Final Works

- **Electrical Finishing:** Ensure all electrical installations are completed and up to code. This includes installing light fixtures, ceiling fans, and outlets, as well as integrating smart home features like lighting control, security systems, or sound systems. Test all electrical components to ensure everything functions properly.

- **Plumbing Completion:** Finalize the plumbing system by installing faucets, sinks, toilets, showers, and bathtubs. Make sure all fixtures are properly connected and free of leaks. Test hot water systems, ensure adequate water pressure, and verify that everything meets local plumbing regulations.

- **Appliances and Fixtures:** Install major appliances, such as ovens, refrigerators, washers, and dryers, and ensure they are correctly connected to the plumbing and electrical systems. Choose high-quality, energy-efficient models that complement your home's style and maximize functionality.

Finishing touches like furniture, decor, and final electrical/plumbing work are essential in creating a functional and aesthetically pleasing living space. Thoughtful selection and attention to detail in these areas will ensure a harmonious and comfortable home environment.

POST CONSTRUCTION

Plan Garden Design (e.g., Lawn, Flower Beds, Trees)

- **Lawn:** A well-maintained lawn can be the foundation of your garden, offering a clean, open space for outdoor activities or relaxation. Choose a grass variety suited to your climate and soil type, and consider whether you want a low-maintenance option like fescue or a more luxurious grass like Kentucky bluegrass.
- **Flower Beds:** Design flower beds that enhance your home's exterior with color and texture. Consider seasonal blooms to ensure year-round visual appeal, and plan a mix of perennials and annuals for longevity and variety. Native plants often require less maintenance and can be more resilient to local weather conditions.
- **Trees and Shrubs:** Trees can provide shade, privacy, and aesthetic appeal. When selecting trees, consider their mature size, growth rate, and how they will complement your overall landscape design. Trees like oaks or maples are great for shade, while smaller, ornamental trees like cherry blossoms or magnolias can add color and visual interest. Shrubs can be used for borders or hedges, adding layers and structure to your garden.

Build Terraces, Decks, and Driveways

- **Terraces:** A terrace provides a flat, usable outdoor space for dining, entertaining, or relaxing. When designing your terrace, consider the materials that best suit your home's style and your climate, such as stone, brick, or pavers. Plan for seating areas, outdoor furniture, and even features like fire pits or outdoor kitchens for added functionality.
- **Decks:** A deck can extend your living space and create a seamless transition from indoors to outdoors. Choose durable materials like wood or composite, and design it to complement your home's architecture. Railings, lighting, and built-in seating can elevate the design and make it more functional.
- **Driveways:** The driveway is a key element of your home's curb appeal. Whether you opt for asphalt, concrete, or decorative pavers, ensure that it is durable and well-drained to withstand weather conditions. Incorporate landscaping around the driveway with borders or greenery to soften the hardscape and create an inviting entrance.

POST CONSTRUCTION

Conduct a Final Inspection of the House

- **Comprehensive Walkthrough:** Before the final handover, conduct a thorough walkthrough of the entire property. This includes checking every room, utility, and system (e.g., plumbing, electrical, HVAC) to ensure that everything is in working order and matches the agreed-upon specifications. Pay attention to finishes, fittings, and fixtures to spot any cosmetic issues like paint touch-ups or poorly installed hardware.
- **Structural Integrity:** Check the overall structural quality of the house, including walls, windows, doors, and the foundation. Ensure that there are no cracks, gaps, or issues with insulation, weatherproofing, or sealing.
- **Functional Tests:** Test all appliances, light switches, outlets, and plumbing fixtures to ensure they operate properly. This also includes running the heating and cooling systems, testing water pressure, and ensuring hot water works throughout the house.

Address Any Deficiencies

- **Punch List:** Create a detailed punch list of any outstanding issues or defects that need to be addressed before finalizing the project. This could include minor cosmetic problems, incomplete installations, or necessary repairs.
- **Follow-Up:** Work with your contractor to ensure that any deficiencies are fixed promptly. Be sure that these corrections meet your standards before signing off on the completion of the work. It's advisable to withhold final payment until all issues are resolved.

POST CONSTRUCTION

Plan and Organize the Move-In

- **Moving Logistics:** Schedule movers and arrange for transportation of your furniture, appliances, and personal items. Consider hiring professional movers or renting moving vehicles to streamline the process. Create a detailed checklist to help with organizing, packing, and labeling.
- **Utility Setup:** Ensure that utilities such as electricity, water, gas, internet, and waste services are connected and ready for use before the move-in date. Update your billing addresses and set up any necessary service appointments, such as for internet installation.
- **Interior Setup:** Once you've moved in, start by arranging essential rooms like the kitchen, bedrooms, and bathrooms. Unpack gradually, starting with the most important items. Organize furniture and decor to suit the flow of your new home.
- **Security and Safety:** Set up home security systems if applicable and change the locks or rekey the house for additional security. Ensure that smoke detectors, carbon monoxide alarms, and fire extinguishers are installed and functioning properly.

The final inspection and move-in phase is the culmination of your home-building journey. Careful planning and attention to detail will help ensure a smooth transition into your new home.

MOVING NOTES

THE MOVING CHECKLIST

Logistics:

- ◯ Set a moving budget
- ◯ Choose a moving company
- ◯ Book movers and truck (if needed)
- ◯ Schedule moving day off work (and for helpers, if applicable)

Purge and Pack:

- ◯ Declutter ruthlessly (donate, or sell)
- ◯ Gather packing supplies (boxes, tape, labels)
- ◯ Research packing hacks for efficiency
- ◯ Start packing non-essentials in labeled boxes (room by room)

New Place:

- ◯ Research your new neighborhood
- ◯ Measure doorways and furniture for fit at your new home
- ◯ Schedule utility and internet transfer/installation for new home

Change of Address:

- ◯ Submit Change of Address (USPS)

Update Your Contact Information:

- ◯ Work & School
- ◯ Family & Friends

Utilities & Home Services:

- ◯ Electricity
- ◯ Water
- ◯ Gas
- ◯ Internet, Phone & Cable
- ◯ Garbage Removal
- ◯ Lawn Service
- ◯ Move-out Cleaning

Finances:

- ◯ Bank
- ◯ Credit Cards
- ◯ Loan Agencies

Subscriptions & Memberships

- ◯ Gym, Clubs & Organizations
- ◯ Streaming Services
- ◯ Online Shopping Accounts

Insurances & Service Providers

- ◯ Homeowner & Renters Insurance
- ◯ Car Insurance
- ◯ Health & Dental Insurance
- ◯ Life Insurance
- ◯ Doctors, Dentists & Veterinarians
- ◯ Accountants
- ◯ Attorneys

Government Agencies:

- ◯ Update your address with DMV
- ◯ Voter Registration
- ◯ Internal Revenue Service (IRS)
- ◯ Social Security Administration

THE MOVING CHECKLIST

PACK AN OVERNIGHT BAG (DAY BEFORE)

Essentials for your first night

- ◯ Pajamas & Change of Clothes
- ◯ Toiletries & Medications
- ◯ Phone Charger & Power Bank
- ◯ Snacks & Drinks
- ◯ Paper Towels & Toilet Paper

LABEL AN OPEN FIRST BOX (DAY BEFORE)

Essential Unpacking Items

- ◯ Trash Bags & Cleaning Supplies
- ◯ Tools (Screwdriver, Multi-Tool)
- ◯ Flashlight & Headlamp
- ◯ Bottled Water & Snacks
- ◯ Medications
- ◯ Dishes, Utensils & Paper Plates
- ◯ Bedding (Sheets, Blanket, Pillow)

MOVING DAY

Preparation:

- ◯ Have cash on hand for moving crew tips and unexpected costs
- ◯ Clear walkways and driveways for movers' access
- ◯ Disassemble furniture (if not done by movers)

Oversee the Move:

- ◯ Double-check inventory list
- ◯ Direct movers where to place boxes in your new home

Settling In:

- ◯ Unpack your labeled "Open First" box and overnight bag
- ◯ Set up the kitchen and bedrooms first for immediate comfort
- ◯ Make sure all utilities are turned on

NOTES:

- ◯ ....
- ◯ ....
- ◯ ....
- ◯ ....
- ◯ ....
- ◯ ....
- ◯ ....

POST CONSTRUCTION

Create a Maintenance Plan for the House and Garden

- **Routine House Maintenance:** Develop a regular schedule for essential home maintenance tasks. This includes checking HVAC systems, replacing air filters, inspecting the roof for leaks or damage, cleaning gutters, and servicing appliances like the water heater. It's also important to periodically inspect windows and doors for drafts and make any necessary repairs to maintain energy efficiency.

- **Garden and Landscaping Maintenance:** Set up a seasonal garden maintenance plan to care for your lawn, flower beds, and trees. This could include regular mowing, fertilizing, pruning, and weeding. In colder climates, plan for winterizing your garden by covering plants, shutting off outdoor water sources, and protecting landscaping from frost.

Obtain Insurance (Home, Liability, etc.)

- **Home Insurance:** Ensure your home is fully insured against risks such as fire, theft, and natural disasters. Review different coverage options to protect the structure, your belongings, and any additional features like pools or outdoor buildings. Consider replacement cost insurance, which covers the cost of repairing or replacing your home without depreciation.

- **Liability Insurance:** Purchase liability insurance to protect against accidents that may occur on your property, such as injuries to guests. This can safeguard you from legal or medical expenses in the event of accidents.

- **Additional Coverage:** Depending on your location, you may want to consider supplemental policies for specific risks, such as flood or earthquake insurance. Also, review your home warranty (if applicable) to understand what repairs or replacements are covered in the first few years after move-in.

POST CONSTRUCTION

Get to Know the Neighborhood and Your Local Community

- **Meet Your Neighbors:** Take time to introduce yourself to neighbors and become familiar with the people around you. This can create a sense of community and offer a support network for things like recommendations for local services, neighborhood safety, and more.
- **Local Services and Amenities:** Learn about nearby schools, grocery stores, parks, healthcare facilities, and other essential services. Familiarizing yourself with these locations will help you settle in faster and make day-to-day tasks more convenient.
- **Community Involvement:** Explore opportunities to engage with your community, such as joining local clubs, attending events, or volunteering. Community involvement not only helps you integrate but also builds a sense of belonging and connection to your new home environment.

The post-move-in phase is about creating a smooth transition into your new life while ensuring your home stays in excellent condition and you feel connected to your new surroundings.

POST CONSTRUCTION

CHAPTER

7

PLANNERS

HOME BUILDING WORKBOOK

ANNUAL TRACKER

JANUARY	FEBRUARY	MARCH
APRIL	**MAY**	**JUNE**
JULY	**AUGUST**	**SEPTEMBER**
OCTOBER	**NOVEMBER**	**DECEMBER**

MONTHLY PLANNER

MONTH OF: _____

1	2	3	4	5	6
7	8	9	10	11	12
13	14	15	16	17	18
19	20	21	22	23	24
25	26	27	28	29	30/31

WEEKLY PLANNER

WEEK OF: _____

SUNDAY

MONDAY

TUESDAY

WEDNESDAY

THURSDAY

FRIDAY

SATURDAY

NOTES

DAILY PLANNER

TODAY'S PRIORITIES

1 _____

2 _____

3 _____

DATE: _____

IMPORTANT REMINDERS

_____

_____

_____

_____

_____

_____

TODAYS SCHEDULE

8:00 AM

9:00 AM

10:00 AM

11:00 AM

12:00 PM

1:00 PM

2:00 PM

3:00 PM

4:00 PM

5:00 PM

6:00 PM

6:00 PM

7:00 PM

8:00 PM

DO TO LIST

MORNING

AFTERNOON

EVENING

NOTES

CHAPTER 8

USEFUL LINKS & RESOURCES

LINKS & RESOURCES

Here's a list of links and resources that can be valuable for your home building adventure:

Architectural and Design Inspiration

- Houzz: **www.houzz.com** - For design inspiration, professional advice, and product recommendations.
- Pinterest: **www.Pinterest.com** – A platform for visual inspiration on home designs, layouts, and decor.
- Architectural Digest: **www.ArchitecturalDigest.com** – Magazine featuring high-end home designs and trends.
- Dwell: **www.dwell.com**
- Home and Garden Magazine: **www.homesandgardens.com**
- ArchDaily: **www.archdaily.com**

Building Codes and Regulations

- International Code Council (ICC): **www.iccsafe.org** – Provides information on building codes and standards.
- National Association of Home Builders (NAHB): **www.nahb.org** – Resources on building standards, regulations, and best practices.

Budgeting and Financing

- Zillow Mortgage Calculator: **www.Zillow.com** – Tool to estimate mortgage payments and compare loan options.
- Bankrate Mortgage Calculator: **www.Bankrate.com** – Another tool for calculating mortgage payments and comparing rates.

Finding Contractors and Services

- Angi (formerly Angie's List): **www.Angi.com** – Find and review local contractors and home service providers.
- HomeAdvisor: **www.homeadvisor.com** – Connect with local professionals for home improvement and repairs.
- Thumbtack – **www.thumbtack.com**

LINKS & RESOURCES

Sustainable Building Practices
- U.S. Green Building Council (USGBC): **www.usgbc.org** – Information on LEED certification and green building practices.
- Energy Star: **www.energystar.gov** – Tips on energy-efficient products and practices for homes.
- Energy.gov – **www.energy.gov**
- Green Building Advisor – **www.greenbuildingadvisor.com**

Interior Design and Decor
- Etsy: **www.BACKtoBASICSpillows.etsy.com** - cute pillows or pillow covers
- Etsy: **www.BACKtoBASICSinterior.etsy.com** - custom home decor
- Etsy: **www.BACKtoBASICSdigital.etsy.com** - instant download checklists
- Better Homes & Gardens – **www.bhg.com**
- The Spruce: **www.thespruce.com** – Ideas on home decorating and design.

DIY and Home Improvement Tips
- This Old House: **www.ThisOldHouse.com** – DIY home improvement advice and tutorials.
- Garden Design – **www.gardendesign.com**

Legal and Contractual Resources
- Building Codes Assistance Project (BCAP) – **www.bcapcodes.org**
- Local Building Department Websites: Look for your local city or county building department's website for specific regulations and permit information.

Home Maintenance
- HouseLogic: **www.HouseLogic.com** – Home maintenance tips and advice.

Move-in Planning & Home Services
- TaskRabbit – **www.taskrabbit.com**
- Thumbtack – **www.thumbtack.com**

"

A home is not just a place,
it's a feeling. Build it with
love and it will last a
lifetime.

-Unknown-

CLOSING STATEMENT

Congratulations on completing your journey through this home building workbook. By meticulously planning each step, from inspiration and design to final move-in, you've laid a solid foundation for creating a space that truly reflects your vision and values. Remember, building a home is more than just constructing walls—it's about crafting a sanctuary where memories are made and dreams come to life.

With the knowledge and tools provided, you're well-equipped to turn your dream into reality. Embrace the process with patience and excitement, knowing that each decision and detail brings you closer to your ideal home.

May your new home be a place of joy, comfort, and endless possibilities. Here's to a successful build and many happy years ahead!

To new beginnings,

Ulli Karner

HOME BUILDING WORKBOOK

_____
_____
_____
_____
_____
_____
_____
_____
_____
_____
_____
_____
_____
_____
_____
_____
_____
_____
_____
_____
_____

"

Building a home is not just
about the present;
it's about crafting a
foundation for a future filled
with memories and
possibilities.

-Ulli Karner-

Made in the USA
Columbia, SC
06 December 2024

48561257R00050